INSIDE
&
OUT
POEMS BY
STEPHEN
LEWANDOWSKI

THE CROSSING PRESS
Trumansburg, New York 14886

Acknowledgments:

Allegany Poetry, Am-Pol Eagle (Buffalo), Applecart, Bachy, Beams: 10X10, Bleb, Blue Cloud Quarterly, Buffalo Courier-Express, Dacotah Territory, Earth's Daughters, The Falcon, Glassworks, Grapevine, Greenfield Review, Hanging Loose, Jeopardy, Juice, Kudzu, Loon, Milwaukee Bugle, Montana Gothic, Northwest Passage, Poetry Now, Quarterly of Polish Heritage, Rapport, Rochester Democrat & Chronicle, road/house, Rolling Stone, Sailing The Road Clear, Scree, Snowy Egret, Some Things Make Us Strong, Star Web Paper, 10X10, Uroboros, Washout Review, Westigan Review, WIN, Wind, Zahir are magazines that printed some of these poems.

Some of these poems originally appeared in chapbooks: *Whispering Grass* from Farmers Museum Press, *Visitor* from White Pine Press, and *Water* from Allegany Mountain Press.

Cover drawing is *Pussy Willows* (watercolor) by Charles E. Burchfield from Munson-Williams-Proctor Institute, Utica, N.Y.

Graphics: Tom Parker

Photograph by Sally Mills/Geoff Tesch

This project is supported by a grant from the National Endowment for the Arts in Washington, D.C. a Federal Agency.

CONTENTS

Inside

& Out—Fall

Winter

INSIDE

open the door
pine trees need not move
to enter the room

ANTON & ANNA LEWANDOWSKI

Grandfather handled steel as
roller-man in the Tonawanda mills.
Introduced my father to the men on his shift
"This is my youngest son Stanley"
& gave him a quarter to bring a pail
of beer from the corner tavern
to wash down their tin box lunches.
I only remember him
as a slight man in skivvies,
rumors of his long dying &
my father coming back to the car—
face gone pale, blue eyes set.
But memory can only affirm the past
& I want no such affirmation.
I know my life flows.
I can no more bring you to life again
than I could calm my fear of your wife,
Anna my grandmother, who spoke Polish
too loud, too quick, would grab at me.
She was crying; she wanted to hold
her grand-child to her breast.
Blood of her blood. Blood of my blood.
What caused that shrinking?
I was raised in another place,
another time, among cold people.
Coolness haunts me grandmother. Cure me.
Hold me. When was the last time I saw you?
Blood whispers through my dreams.
It has a life of its own, which I ask
my share of. Speak to me, my heart.
I'll understand where the words come from.

ARBOR VITAE

"The natives make their plates of sweet wood."

—Raleigh

You come out
looking around.
Birds teeter in the branches,
fish balance above your crib,
amusement for sweet Cedar.
Out of earth & water & air
you made a long journey.
Birds row past.
What seems precarious
in their lives
is sure.
Your slate gray eyes
& lots of tan hair
are colors of the waxwing,
birds which nest
where they please—
crested troupe of
tumblers & acrobats
working the swaying,
resinous branch ends.
Cedar sticks out her tongue
& glances at me.
Be sure.
Eye & taste the world
& find it sweet o sweet.

7

THE CORN PALACE

for Harley Elliott

"You had to be there."

How glad I am we stopped
in the home of George McGovern.
This was before McGovern was anything
but Senator, before his incredible
faultering run for the Presidency.
I'm told Mitchell was established in May 1879,
connected to the railroad in September 1880,
and numbered 1200 souls by 1882.
In that Dakota "every townsite was a city,
every creek a river, every crop
a bonanza, every breeze a zephyr,
and every man a damned liar."
In the nearby Red River Valley
Paul Bunyan was being invented.
Men were running, walking, driving,
being driven West then, hurrying
against the seasons & the locusts
to get a first crop of wheat
into the broken prairie.
Now it's corn & Indian trinkets.
All those plastic mocassins
fabricated at nearby reservations.
The shelves piled high with
Korean Indian trinkets.
We can't afford to buy Japanese
Indian artifacts anymore so I suppose
they keep the whole stock to themselves.

What do we have to give
            for these beads & mirrors?
What do we *have* to give?
The corn, at least, is real,
all natural earth colors, even blue.
Murals set in the walls of this
remodeled gymnasium glow with corn life.
The extravagant Byzantine exterior
only whets our corn appetite.
Our guide says men create
            the murals fresh each year
                        but I know better.
Late at night I see the string of black ants,
a huge army passing single file through
the doors of the Corn Palace
each one bearing in its mandibles
a single kernel of gaudy corn.

FOR YOU

"Kabir says: Fantastic! Don't let a chance like this go by!"

On the couch
both of us feel like high school.
That is, the touching
is urgent but restrained.
The couch has this aspect as
surely as it has little legs
carved like lions.
We travel upstairs
where the bedrooms begin
& slip out of our skins.
The palm of my hand
collects the flesh of your breast
like water in the hollow of a rock.
Hands, you're on your own now.
I want it dark
so I can see through my fingers.
But you say you get
confused in the dark.
I'm nervous to be naked
before you, some fine animal.
In the morning we won't
have to make choices.
The sun comes up with
all its light on new snow.
My window faces east.

INSUBORDINATION

"You who don't believe me,
  try saying no."

Fired from a job again
because I'll say yes or no
just as it strikes me,
not as I'm instructed.
The socialworker shuffles the cards.
I wish I could say he smiles but
he smirks. He says
"These are all possibilities,
now what do you want?"
If this was a game I'd play
with the hand I'm dealt.
If I could begin again I'd work
with my hands forming wood, earth,
stone, clay or fiber into
essentials: food, clothes or shelter.
Got any job like that?
The real work is always there.
Sometimes we're paid one way;
sometimes another; sometimes
we have to pay. Take care
of yourself. This is the way.

KLIPNOCKIE

There's an Indian head painted in the front window.
Up front of the arch some young guys play pool.
Older folks play pitch in the back.
"I won't even tell you what the other name is."
The one in workclothes is loosening up for the night shift.
He's trying to get his arm around the waist
of a fat woman in bobby sox.
"Are you students? I worked
forty years a janitor at the college."
I denied it. Outside a thin snow began falling.
No stools at the bar, it's built for leaning,
elbow groove, one foot on the brass rail.
Booths are built in at one side, under a trio
of mounted animals: lake trout, moose head, loon.
Deer heads, 8 point buck and 4 point, gaze
down from other walls; one, because of the light,
seems about to speak.
Rheingold, the defunct NYC beer,
advertises from the quaint Southwest,
a balky burro, you know the type.
Hank Williams breaks
"Your Cheatin' Heart" on the jukebox
the millionth time since his death.
An old fella tells me the shad don't run
as far up as Delhi, though I might get some
at a little store south of Andes.
A rugged woman tends the bar, mopping up,
serving the draughts, shots and food—
pickled eggs, chips, herring and crackers.
She looks up and smiles each time to the drunk's
"Hello my little hickory nut!"

THE NATURE OF MEDITATION

Something was stirring then
but it didn't come forward.
This was a translation.
Some insect gnawing at green leaf tissue.
Some particle of sand cleft by frost.
Let the clods in the field,
whole galaxies fall apart.
This thought is indivisible.
Eater & eaten are one.
Growth & grower are one.
The animate enlivens
the inanimate, briefly.

Scrub off the dirt &
let the carrot shine through.

NISKEYUNA

"Anything may with strict propriety be
called perfect which perfectly answers
the purpose for which it was designed."

Shaker Rule

Standing in the shop, surrounded
by wood-working machines, saws
and lathes, hand tools, and boxes
of fitted slats and rungs to be
shaped into chairs, he spoke with us.
I forget what we said, but his hand
was on the back of a pine chair,
rubbing, slowly rubbing the finish;
he spoke slowly, old man, few words.
He rested his hand on that chair.

POEMS MUST SPEAK TRUTH

for Gerald McCarthy

The poet who came back from Viet Nam
writes about his buddy who did not:
"you black bastard, all shot to shit."
He says that none of us
try hard enough
to tell the truth.
Will the truth make us free,
or will we just laugh?
Laughter's our bondage
& our freedom.

At the Abbey of the Genesee
colored light streams through
the deeply inset, stained glass windows.
The chapel's dark except for their light
& for the one spotlight on the altar.
We tourists pass through the back
in shadows. When the young monk
hunched in the dark pews
turns his face to us
it's twisted with his crying.

What is the worth of telling this truth?
What power shall we speak it to?

SPEAKING ENGLISH

after Juan Ramon Jimenez

Letters are stitches
on the written page.
I wear language like the second-hand
green railroad workshirt with
frayed cuffs & collar.
My thanks to the Salvation Army.

I balance
the comfort of speaking with
the need to keep still.

Speaking is wearing the shirt.
In stillness, the body grows
until the seams fly apart.

SPELLS

for Michael Corr

Elm branches rap against the roof.
Deep green light coming in the window
is filtered through leaves.
Since early morning,
since shaving in the wavering
glass framed atop the dresser,
my distraction has been growing.
The mirror disfigured me;
my razor drew blood.
I turned the mirror to the wall and
walked outside to split some kindling.

A moon, white as a forehead,
rises through the branches.
I look up from my work;
it's late at night;
I don't remember dusk.
Feathery tree limbs
wave toward the sky.
Moths with faces inscribed on their wings
begin their annual flight to the moon.
Pansies rustle in their bed.
Barred with trees' shadows
a moonlit road leads away.
If I were to follow tonight
buried treasures would shine
out of the earth, blue,
to distract me.

I walk indoors and gaze
at the freshly swept floor.
Broad, interlocking oak boards
worn down at the threshold.
You come to my door
and, without a word, smile.
The old woman's in your face.
My house is in order.
I fly out into the moonlight.

PLANT TALK

Twice now I've heard my mother say
how you should be the centerpiece
for a Japanese flower arrangement.
I tell her they don't use live plants,
but she's right about your form:
spare, nearly all graceful stem stretching
toward two new leaves unfolding and
two buds, horns set at right angles to the stem.
You're working hard to bring the leaves'
shiny green surfaces into direct sunlight;
from the back we see the red feathering veins.
Only your name would be wrong
beefsteak begonia.

LANDOWNER

My house will be built
with lumber from trees
on the property, local wood.
When wind blows over the hill
and groans down the chimney flue,
the house will creak, knot and grain,
rough planed boards in sympathy
for trees bowing
to the storm.

FIT

I am the person
my parents warned me against.

Always dressed me in clothes
4 sizes too big, "don't worry,
you'll grow into them
before they wear out."
Shirt sleeves rolled back once
& buttoned inside out,
pant cuffs wearing at the heel.
When I was sixteen I began
to insist on clothes
I liked & which fit.

But now, at 30 & some
I find I'm becoming more &
more just like them as
I remember them from my childhood.
Mother's gesture resides in my wrist.
Father's blue eye stares out;
his baldness creeps across my skull.

Going through the family album
I find my likeness in
this uncle with his fishpole,
that grandfather dressed for his wedding.

It's a way of carrying the flesh,
how well it fits the bones.

Can I outgrow death, split
the seams of my life before
it's worn out?

I'm watching the old people keenly
for they are growing into their deaths,
a perfect fit, which, one day
will be mine.

AGAIN

No coincidences, no accidents

Taking a lover again
makes me close my eyes &
sink in upon myself.
Not asleep but waiting
The taste is delicious, yes,
moreso after years without.
Sadness evaporates like the mist
it is before the morning sun.
We chase it all out, loving.
Do I lose my aloneness
the poet advised me to cultivate?
How could I? Listen
the words come up from a new space!
I open my eyes this morning
on a fresh world.
Coming downstairs
we find an oriole trapped
on the glassed-in side porch.
I mean it no harm
but the bird doesn't know.
Finally catching & holding
I stroke its brilliance &
the bird doesn't fight.
I open the door &
open my hand &
the bird leaps upward
in a gold streak.

67 PLYMOUTH VALIANT

Just after I lost my license, she left me &
the two events got mixed up in my mind &
I thought it would never run again.
But now some of you have heard,
maybe even cruised in my growler.
I gave it oil & a jump & it turned over.
The state blesses orange & black.
Tags adhere to the clear windshield.
I stuck an eternal knot in one window &
a decal map of the State of Washington
(Olympics & Cascades) in another.
A plastic Buddha, if I had one, would ride the dash.
I thought my garage would always be full.
I thought it would sit in the rest
of my life's driveway & bleed rust.
        I thought   I thought
Now it's out. Here it is carrying me.
The rest of my life's riding in the back seat.
Quiet back there! My tent's in the trunk.
The gas lamp wants to come along.
You there, you ready? Let's go.

& OUT/FALL

Hay's no good but
the bales are perfect.

ALMANAC

Land plowed and harrowed,
the yearly crop of rocks gathered,
we planted our cleared acres
in corn, six kernels to the hill.
At the waxing moon, my wife and I made love
in the fields, lying between rows of golden
green corn shoots; the next night we stayed
in bed and thought of our children, unborn.
Praised the cornstalks' straightness in June,
prayed for rain, and saw them tassel at top,
kernels white and even as baby teeth filling the cob.
Silk grown dark on the ears,
we ate all we could in July & August:
corn with every meal, roasting the toughest,
and put the remainder away in September—
mason jars in the dug-out back cellar.
Seed ears hung against the shed
dried in the October sun.
Braided husks we wove into crowns
and masks to change our faces.

Through long winter nights
we inhabit this farmhouse,
climbing stairs to sleep.
Descending at dawn
we recognize the hanging
masks from our dreams.

LABOR DAY

You built the shed.
Though your fine old table saw
crusted with sawdust & oil
must rip easily through these oak boards,
you stand puzzling over the bill.
We have loaded a ton of fragrant
wood on the bed of our pick-up.
The figures & names are labor for you.
Your son plays in the sawdust pile behind
the shed. Your wife yells from the house.
Sparrows are building in the storm windows,
tires, rough planks, and radiators
stored in the shed's rafters.
From below we see their mud & feathers
& long pieces of twine hanging down.
The farm is not fertile—
rocks sprout through the soil,
but your house garden does well.
She's weeding it now, throwing up
weeds & mud, hair tied back under a bandana.
The planer stands in a pile of curled shavings.
The huge cast iron stove is cold but ready.
Fertilizer bags full of UC cans lean
against your desk. Wood you've got.
Forest takes more of Italy Valley each year.
Russ, we'll help you with that bill.
Let us do the spelling out & adding up.
Your works are good; do what you do best.

THE SCHOLAR CHOPS WOOD

Set block up on a firm base.
Standard cord: 4' by 4' by 8'
Face cord: 4' high by 8' long by 12-18" wide,
    convenient for stoves.
Handle curves in my hands.
If the wood is properly seasoned,
cut a year in advance and stored in shelter,
seek to burn shad bush,
dogwood (small green flowers with showy
white or pink bracts), swamp white oak,
or black locust (fragrant white flowers).
Swing begins in the small of my back.
The heating value of green wood is about
5% less than that of seasoned wood.
One cord (from the Latin for catgut, not
the Latin for heart or the Spanish for chain)
of seasoned hardwood equals one ton of anthracite
(hard, from the Greek carbuncle) coal.
Wood cut in winter warms twice:
once burning, once chopping.
The average upstate NY farm family would use
50 face cords per year for heating and cooking.
Handle flexes slightly; blade bites.
A ton of hardwood ashes contains
1000 lb. calcium carbonate, 130 lb.
potash, and 30 lb. phosphoric acid.
Blade runs along the grain.
Because they lack nitrogen, wood ashes
(from the Old English *aesce*, to burn)
are best used on sour land seeded to
alfalfa (from the Arabic al-fasfasah)
or clover (from the Germanic *klaibron*).
White wood falls away.

BEYOND THE EQUINOX

Leaving my friends' home & fire
built in the stove, the cold
turns a latch deep in my stomach.
From this night onward
leaves will fall from the trees.
They'll turn & fall.
Clear sky: first frost.
Clear sky: star's singular brilliance
& the Milky Way looking like the path
our ancestors journeyed down.
I head toward home.
Driving Castle Road I think of Seneca
palisades in maple forest clearings.
But I look out on flat fields of
unharvested beets, cabbage, beans.
Places, an eight-foot wall of
cornstalks encloses the road.
Heavy ears hang down as if
inviting the International picker.
The land swells & flows under
the car like music, like water.
The land stills my heart which speeds
at the center of a metal mass.
Isolated farmhouses, their lights
remind me of the lives within.
Seasons turn & my life turns with them.
I follow the road leading to the village
the Seneca called "place where we live."
Only the sight of a falling star
slows my rush toward home.

THOUGHTS ON FALL PLOWING

"And he gave it for his opinion, that whoever could make two ears of corn, or two blades of grass, to grow upon a spot of ground where only one grew before, would deserve better of mankind, and do more essential service to his country, than the whole race of politicians put together."

Gulliver's Travels

plowed in September & fitted for winter wheat
plowed in November, bare black earth under snow

not only does "plowed down sillion shine" but
reflects, patches of blue sky in the furrows

plowed this morning, snow in the afternoon,
at dusk snow nests in behind the clods

"couldn't work this field otherwise"

sky opens & shuts
clouds rapidly sliding over
snow in the wind

heated cab & long johns
hooded sweatshirt & good boots

geese drift down like falling leaves
into corn stubble

tractor tire ruts full of ice—
vast machine effort to move
makes a mirror

watching for mice flushed
red fox stands by
flourishing his tail
unafraid while the machine runs
tape deck in the cab plays
Stevie Wonder's "Living for the City"

Dewitt rides the tractor clockwise
six bottoms behind
turning up red clay
so frost will have a crack at it

waves in land last longer

WIND BEFORE DAWN

Flapping at four o'clock
What can rattle rattles.
The wind throws itself around
like a willful child. It's easy
to attribute emotions to the elements
on such nights. Bits & pieces of
light things fly through the air.
The weeping willow looming
over my neighbor's house whips
itself furiously, animated by
thousands of airy penitentés.
Gusts batter against dark windows
of the sleeping town; here & there
a limb crashes down, shingles tear off.
Not much to show for such an effort—
"and I'll huff and I'll puff"—
what a time to be visited by wolves.
My old house stirs itself, creaky
joints & joists, stone & brick grinding
& me in my bed then dreaming of sails
& flying through the air, now sitting &
drinking tea in the face of a big wind.

DAY OF THE DEAD

for Ambrose Bierce

This is their day.
There's no escaping it:
the skull will always be chalice-shaped,
a bit of tasty liquor within,
& the bread loaf does suggest
the way dirt mounds over a grave,
headstone melting with its message in the rain.
The backbone is a splendid spit
for shishkabobing these pounds of meat.
Pastries feeling around like fingers
with pink powdered sugar nails.
Agate eyeballs at marbles in the street.
You can't keep a good corpse down—
a tight spring jumps the jack-
in-the-box & he leaps out of the coffin
grinning & nodding & grinning.
We carry armloads of pungent marigolds
for a cushion beside the grave.
The meal's hot, dark & sweet chicken molé
& we bring along enough for many.
Shots of tequila keep us
the living warm tonight.
I ask you friends
where is life carried on? always
in the presence of death.
Be with us.

NOVEMBER 17th

First day of upstate NY's hunting season &
the Phelps diner is full of deer hunters.
A shotgun leans against the pool table.
Story broke this morning: the woman who's spent
her life studying deaths does not believe.
Or rather, believes death is a light &
easy passage from life to life.
As I read this news I am surrounded by men
in orange, red & yellow plastic caps;
they chew rolls hard as statistics &
dip sweet doughnuts in black coffee.

Driving to work we meet a stationwagon on the lake road.
Tied on the fender, a deer gapes and drips
dark blood in streams down the cream finish.

We work under the mountain,
pruning a vineyard, fall work.
The vines grow right up out of rock.
Looking up from our work
we see the mountain's covered
with soft fur of trees.
A few green pines stand out
in the thousands of bare branches.
We hear hunters' guns on the wooded mountain.

Sometimes we're on our knees. We pull off layers
of clothes as the weather clears & warms.
A pair of hawks soar above us.
They cry & hang motionless
sailing into the wind. Gain height.
Suddenly one folds & silent rushes
like death downwind, almost out
of sight behind the mountain.
It wheels, wings grasping updrafts,
hangs again & ascends in spirals.
All day we bent to work in the vineyard,
hunters stalking over the mountain,
hawks slipping through passages in the wind.

WINTER

UNTITLED

snow on cornstalks
snow on teasel & wild carrots
a little snow on an abandoned Gulf Station
snow on suburban lawns
snow in the pines, sifting
snow on a plowed field, in the furrows
snow on signs (hard to read)
pines & dark road resisting snow
snow on red willow (osier) switches in the swamp
snow on an unfinished house, bare rafters
snow in the junkyard, on an auto missing hood & engine
why is Diane's Little Restaurant closed?
spruce burdened by snow, let some of it down
snow on a playing field backstop
snow on three metal siloes
is that winter wheat under the snow?
cows lie down in snow
snow on willow very yellow
snow on Lone Elm Restaurant, its elm cut down
snow in the cemetery: grass & wreaths & stones
why do you disdain the sidewalk?
grey clouds over Rochester meet white clouds off Ontario,
          object: snow
snow on roofs of tract houses, more real than the houses
snow on Genesee River, brown
snow on Barge Canal, gone
can't see snow atop oil tanks
snow on twisted trees against blackened brick building
look up, yes, even snow wisps on War Memorial's
          inverted bomb sculpture
step down from bus, what's this
in my cuff?   snow

SOME THINGS WORK

We use the horse to haul out wood.
He farts before he pulls.
You won't find a tractor'll do that.
The season's too wet for tractors—
they just dig themselves a hole.
All the farmers bitch about their crops,
lost or delayed, puddles in the corn
rows & beans turning black with mold.
But the horse pulls real nice & a load
of sound dead-fall elm & lively hickory
slides up the 1/2 mile hill to the house.
We buzz up the logs, split the biggest
with ax & maul, stove-size.
Some people might get a kick
out of our stone-boat:
dark blue volkswagen hood & chain,
but it holds what a horse can pull
& slips right over the grass
in the low, wet spots.
It works & we work & later
we sit before the fire.

(YOU'RE NEVER) ALONE IN BED

Windows all frozen up
I can't see a thing.
I wear flannel pajamas.
The windows wear these terrific
frost pattern threads.
Outside my room, from the northeast
corner of the farmhouse, electric
cables arc toward the barns.
Wind coming around the corner
hits those lines & strums a chord
which sets my bedsprings shivering.
Vibrations lift me in the night
neither sleeping nor waking but
hovering just inches above the bed,
myselves here & elsewhere
split by overtones
into the one who sleeps
& the one who dreams
& all those others
who go on breathing & beating.
We all roll over.

SEEING AN ALL WHITE DOG IN
MID DECEMBER, STANLEY, NY

Over a ridge near the creek,
palisaded village, timbers 12' high,
orchards chopped down by Sullivan, fall 1779.
The Seneca of Ganundesaga would have known
what you are good for
special dog, apart, for the ceremony
coming with first snows, dark days.
Carry this message of thanks:
we are doing well.
The dog's life you live which,
as we all know, is very fine.
sleep, sniff, scratch,
maybe fight a bit if that's your nature,
follow the hunt, clean up scraps,
watch for intruders.
Healthy, not a spot or blemish.
Maybe your ears *are* a bit too long
but wouldn't you be sad if
tobacco wasn't burned for you?
"who has an old dream?
  who has a new dream?
  who has a white dog?"
Feathers and quills
Five rows of purple beads (that color)
and one row of white
Red paint in spots and lines
Though the uncles must strangle you with cords,
you'll be covered with ribbons,
burned with mint leaves, tobacco,
the adornments!
Our dreams go with you.
We feast.

CNR, NORTHERN ONTARIO, FEBRUARY 24th

For miles we passed nothing but jack pines.
Pines standing, leaning & fallen,
fresh snow in their branches.
Growing crowded close,
their needles plume out at the top.
Not much more than clearings at
Superior Junction & Ghost River:
gov't housing, Bay Co. store, hotel.
The train stopped long enough
at Sioux Lookout to let off
3 Indians (all drunk in the snowdrifts)
and to take on 4 more (not yet).
One announces to the car he's a healer.
Vast stretches of pines sway
together in a light breeze.
Their unison is a hush on the land.
Even our little car world feels
the power of their nodding.
The healer bumps along the aisle
with tied-up packages, "gifts" he says.
The train crosses a bridge over a creek;
we glimpse one set of footprints on the ice.
Coming.   Going.   passed.

MEET THE AX

This is your ax, treat it well.
The ax is not your friend
though it will serve as well
as a simple machine may.
Steel drawn to two edges,
hence double-bitted &
tempered to stay sharp.
Head balances the handle
offering itself to your hands,
curved lines draw-shaved
to a comfortable form
in long grained white ash.
How could I mistake the ax's purpose
or pick it up wrong-end-to?
Rub the head with oil &
never leave the ax out in night dew;
shelter the ax when you sleep.
Like it or not, this winter
the ax is your companion.
Play no philosophical games with it.
Don't ask it to solve your problems.
Chop earnestly, examine the wedge
that holds body & soul of the ax
together. Chips fly away.
This way & that
the ax bites deep.
Throw your body into its stroke;
you grow warm.

NOTHING MUCH

Nothing much going on out here.
Pheasants are picking around
under their favorite apple tree.
The famous poet's left already
bearing off her growing reputation
like a beaver coat with alligator cuffs.
Very heavy & sometimes she forgets it.
Luckily she's got this boyfriend
who picks up after her with a
"Baby, you got this & that?"
He talks about how she's the ambitious one.
We talked about all the people we don't like
who're writing too much, no matter how much.
We talked about where the poets hang out.
After scallion omelettes
they drove off in her large red auto,
the one she demolished in a poem.
I came back inside after waving,
put on the Charlie Parker album loud
so I could hear it upstairs,
gave my cat a shot of catnip
which made her dance in the hall
& sat down with my typewriter.
Settling down, I record
that my typewriter's bluer than the sky,
that wet snow's falling with little wind,
that it sticks wonderfully to trees & bushes,
that the road is a strip of brown one car wide.
I wish them luck on that road.

SPRING

SLEEPING ON THE FLYWAY

We saw black spots
over deepest parts of the lake
where ice broke out in the thaw.
Huge blocks of ice piled up
on the windward shore.
We walked among their blue shapes.
At night the wind coming over Cayuga Lake
rocked our whole house to sleep.
Geese stopped for the night on open water.
All day we had watched their formations
pointing north. In the dusk
their voices came louder as they
dropped down to look the lake over.
Sounds the flock made on the lake
at night glowed the color of perfect
feathers behind their folded wings;
our dreams flushed pearl gray.
They were gone again
before we rose in the morning.

SUCKER BROOK

runs right through
the heart of town.
Full of trash, bald tires,
leaves, & A&P shopping carts.
Spring nights you see
lights down in the stream bed—
kids spear suckers & throw
the dying & dead up on lawns.
Once every ten years
the creek slips its banks
undermining garage walls,
invading neighborhood cellars,
prankishly sweeping away
lawn furniture, leaving
its bed clean & clear.

LETTER TO JOSIE FROM ITHACA

dear Josie—
   I just wanted to say
   WCW wrote the poems that
   need to begin this way.
There are no coincidences.
Glad to stop at your house this morning
for talk of the Brothers Grimm & Rilke.
Glad you've learned to breathe.
Now driving again toward Ithaca,
I watch farmers haul a winter's worth
of manure from barn to field.
It lays in long black ribbons on the snow.
The smell penetrates everywhere.
Saw a sparrowhawk, mouse clutched
in its claws, balancing on a wire.
Saw the interior of a grove of tightly
planted white pines near the army depot.
Stopped to piss that rosehip tea
& sank my feet in the mud. You know,
I mean it about the poem being
what you or I can get away with.
We'll rescue something from
this world yet!
               Steve

COPING

"Today we discuss how to be sexy
  without being sexist"

Here comes a young woman strolling,
her shoulders luminously bare as
aspen bark, long white dress sways
held up by her (as in the opening
chapters of pornographic novels)
ample breasts. I greet her
with a sudden exhalation as if
I were really trying to take her in.
Since we meet in the militant indoor-ness
of the shopping mall, my breath is lost
among the building's breathings.
The young woman scarcely notices
my highly personal vacuum.

I might have said "Here, let me
fall at your feet for a moment. . . . "
I pined after her all the way home—
passing fishermen sunk up to their armpits
in waders in the streams, farmers parked
in the plowed fields, the boxes of
their pick-ups full of the sacks of seed grain—
all the way home with
            the windows of the car
                    rolled down to cool off.

CONVERSATION

"I want it all to pass through me"
I told her & went on to explain
that "all" meant time, words, events
maybe even money flowing as water.
Experience would wash over my life
like Honeoye Creek vaulting down
the rocky falls near my house,
tumbling smooth stone & smoothing ledges.
Currents shape the stream bed;
jewelweed droops over the bank;
tough willows & cottonwoods always grow
back although maimed & uprooted.
I say again "the trick's not to be
an obstruction," not to offer a hold
to forces which would sweep us away
at flood-time. I want to flow in time,
to find form in apt & delectable language.
That night, after making love
in the afternoon, we played at dancing
on the balcony under the full moon.

SASSAFRAS

Shovel (curved blade)
& gloves (leather palm).
Creeping tree spreads underground.
Leaf shaped like a catcher's mitt
comes up through last year's leaves.
Dig down to the knobby root.
You'll only get part
when you start pulling.
Columbus smelled sassafras
far at sea & continued
sailing west.
Champlain & Hudson drank it in 1607.
Raleigh carried some back to England.
DeSoto learned from the Choctaw
to use it in gumbo-filet.
Iroquois drank sassafras spring tonic.
Still do.
Cousin of laurel, sassafras dyes cloths
soft gray, rose-tan, or excellent brown.
Dirt-covered root; washed it becomes
red-skinned; broken open
to white & fragrant
Grate. Dry. Boil. Drink.
Sweat. Piss. Dream.

EASTER SUNDAY

The day clears & darkens
according to its own schedule.
Awoke to new snow this morning,
the valley full of it & dark trees
accentuated against white hillsides.
Trucks gradually cleared the roads
but church-goers walked gingerly anyway,
some new shoes & some shined
old shoes in the melting snow.
Late rising, the day half gone
as I read from Rilke's letter to Lou:
"I waken every morning with a cold shoulder, there,
    where the hand should lay hold that shakes me."

During the afternoon
the sun breaks through
just when
light will be reflected through our windows
from the greenhouse glass.
Reflected sunlight, brilliant &
teeming as water, reaches across the valley
& touches walls of our room.
I'm warmed by the coincidence.
Thanks, but I've had quite enough
of your agitation.
I'm shaking off that cold shoulder
you gave me. Suddenly I'm happy
with an amphibian pleasure
which can't remember why,
forgets who.

APRIL 14

for Edith Shiffert

the small room
the guest room
who is the guest?
making it ready
the guest is coming
the guest's on the way
painted the guest room today
ceiling a flat white over
the old pink in one coat
walls arc Williamsburg green though
I'd swear they taste of mint
bamboo woodwork & door
& the floor, ah floorboards
of rough pine are tan—
cedar color
welcome the guest
the one window's wide open & nesting
blackbirds' music streams in
"your room is still wet" but
we stand outside the door
& look approvingly in

LOOKING INTO THE ROOT CUPBOARD

for Joe Bruchac

The Biological Clock gives another
start, & last year's onions & potatoes
throw up their long, pale arms.
I'm surprised to find so much activity
in such a dark, dry space.
But they power themselves, sugar
in the bulb & starch in the tuber
compelling this reaching up like
prisoners released from the dungeons
at the end of "Fidelio," the result
of faith kept. Nearly blind, they stagger
out clutching one another for support,
feeling with their faces for the sunlight,
arms & hands grasping at the free air.
This scene, though perhaps not so beautifully
orchestrated, must have been repeated recently
in Greece & Spain when the Generals heard
their own time rung out on the Great Clock.

Put into garden rows again
the potatoes will increase their own kind.
For now, the onions are free of the cycle
& if I plant them, it will be solely
to watch them blossom.

50

SUMMER

SLEEPWALKER

A creaking bannister and
a familiar tread on the steps,
he comes down the back stairs;
his eyes are open.

We'd been playing cards, gathered
around a lamp placed in
the center of our kitchen table.
He walks out in his bedclothes.

We were warned not to wake him.
The lake and beach are lit
by an almost full moon.
He stands in the deep lawn
and stretches as if he would wake.
Night noises rise about him.

A breeze stirs the nightgown
against his legs. We can't help
noticing how old he has grown.
We carry blankets to wrap him
should he wake up in the open.
But he's had enough of the night
and whatever draws him out—

he climbs the porch steps
ahead of us, pushes open
the glass paneled door and
enters the bright kitchen.
His feet shine with dew.

WILLOWS

Asleep in this shade
the horses of my dreams
have it their way;
they gallop to you.

REX ANSLEY, NEAR HALL, NY

You'd swear he was expecting
every rock his plow turns up.
I've never seen a man
with such a smile.
He tells us his wife's been sick;
he takes care of her.
His son took him up in an airplane
& he shot pictures of his farm.
He wants to show them to you,
but they're all mixed-in with
the slides of his grand-children.

NIGHT FISHING

for Arthur Augustus Sterling (1870-1957)

Picture me at the side of an old fisherman.
Grandfather is frequently angry;
in tobacco-stained grey cord pants
and a wool shirt; his flying white hair
and bristly chin scare me.
Many years removed, he's my father.
We rock in the boat, oarlocks groaning, for hours.
He blows out cigar smoke with the wind,
spits on his hook, feels
the anchor grind and hold.
Grandfather jerks a fish right into the boat.
A small boy had best stay out
of the way of his long bamboo pole.
He's been a hunter and fisher
for fifty years and remembers every time
he fished this cove and what they caught.
He remembers the day when they took
twenty-five bass on soft-shell crabs.
A bullhead dances up near the Coleman lantern;
gargoyle of a fish, little fury snatched
from the water by twelve pount test,
into our circle of light.
Bullheads croak in the bottom of the boat,
squirming black skin and flashing poison spine.
The light of burning gas shines
shadows deep into a black night.

RETURN

Margins of the garden grew burdock
leaves large enough to hide me.
After dark, I peopled the rooms
upstairs with my nightmares.
Returning now, how tiny
the garden has grown!
how empty the house!

SAUERKRAUT FESTIVAL, PHELPS, NY

Cabbages have a light of their own:
one pile glows the green
of luna moth wings,
the other's wine stain purple.
Heavy trucks roll into town,
their boxes heaped up with
heads to dump on the piles
in front of Silver Floss.
When one escapes the load,
no one bothers to pick it up.
A spilled head unfolds like
a bankroll in the road.
The Princess is chauffeured
through town, smiling & waving
her delicately gloved hands.

FOR FINDING A MEADOWOOD ARROWHEAD

Hopewell, New York

You're made as much of patience as of flint.
Fine fractured edge & deep side notch.
Hard gray tooth for biting animals
at a distance,
your weight in my hand
balances us both.
A great chain of events stands
behind both our presences
& our meeting here.
I feel your maker's hand
in mine.
A plow scars the earth.
Like a bad penny
you rise through the furrow.

RIPPING TREES OUT

ash dogwood maple sassafras
basswood   pin cherry   willow
poplar   quaking aspen   cottonwood
Am I pining away? Not in these woods.
As the tractor pulls a limb off the huge oak,
I'm seeing you undressing in the darkened
bedroom. Clean white wood appears
as the bark sleeve slips away.
That limb is strong. But it will break.

Sadness wells up in me
like sap rising in a maple.
Thinking of you again
sweetness washes over the wounds.

SENECA CASTLE, N. Y.

They've cut down two
of the village's largest trees:
locusts of a 4' diameter which
must have looked on while
the Seneca built their palisades
by the banks of Flint Creek.
The trees had given up
over the years
on the idea of foliage &
channeled all their energies
into the massive trunks now
sectioned, split & parceled out
among the neighbors.
Under dark, fissured bark
locust flesh is white & sweet.
Messy job, butchering a great tree
lying in its chips & sawdust like
a fleshed-out whale in its blood.
White sticks of wood are thrown
around the yard, waiting to be
stacked & seasoned, later burned.

GARDENER

Say—

    you are a seventy-five year old widow,
your husband gone these fifteen years,
and you keep up the house and grounds
yourself.

Say—

    the fairy ring appears on your lawn
one morning. Will you be frightened?
Rings have lasted a thousand years.
It's a blemish on your property.
Your lawn must be uniformly green.
You wouldn't wear a spotted dress.
I'm your man.

GRASS

Grass will always remind me of you.
Grass & the prairie flowers you showed me:
larkspur, falling star, blue-eyed grass.
That strip of virgin prairie at the park
meant something to you, something about
an eternal fragility I could never handle.
One time I remember you wrote
in a letter about jumping out of the car &
the tall grass reaching up to your nipples.
Ever since I've been dreaming about your breasts;
sometimes there's grass; always my hands close in sleep.

But I continue walking on lawns, even cutting
& trimming grass for homeowners, for pay.
I pull out stems to look them up in the book.
This country I come from was once covered
all with forests, no grass. Of trees,
I love the elm best. What are my hands
in the dreams closing over? Do I kiss?
Grass will always remind me of you.

USEFUL BLOSSOMS

"Reach me a gentian, give me a torch."

—D. H. Lawrence, "Bavarian Gentians"

Along the wall I plant Mammoth Russian
sunflower seeds from a colorful Burpee pack.
In a circle I plant winged marigold seeds
given me by Chris & Heather just days before
their wedding (almost wrote 'weeding').

Be my prayer wheel sunflower.
I love your changes &
plant to set you turning
as the planets move.
Your patience is rooted
in the soil & reminds me
of the heart's necessary
turning in love & good intent.
The great head grows so heavy
it bends the stem down
among heart-shaped leaves.

I know I'll have to get my hands dirty
to change the tire on my car.
The Dharma's Wheel is a ring of fire,
not so easily handled.

Marigolds begin to bloom in June through
fingery leaves & continue straight on
through October; yellow & glowing orange &
my favorites the gold with blood
red centers & frilly edges.

As the hundreds of flowers composing
the sunflower's center dry up & blow away,
I see rows of black & white seeds.
They ripen outward in.
Out of the sunflower's heart
comes seeds striped like clowns.
Meanwhile, from the circle rises
a penetrating smell of marigolds
which is their music.

SURVEYING THE MILITARY TRACT

for Barbara Graymont

Remembering George, Father
of this country's noblest geometry,
we establish uprightness.
An àir bubble caught in a tube
desires to rejoin its sky-brothers.
Putting out proper alignments
& portions: section, quarter-section,
the back forty all in buckwheat.
We settle a border dispute advanced
to the courts of law. What we say, goes.
The participants will their grudges to
their sons & sons' sons. The land stays.
We establish that ownership ends here.

The scope projects my eye-beams.
Yes, there he is, holding a rod
& smiling through his wooden teeth.
He plants the rod firm on the ground &
against his thigh & it begins
to sprout twigs & leaves.
It blossoms; his beard grows out.
The tree's decorated with numbers,
stripes & waves twelve feet high in the air.
I comprehend an acre.
We do not observe but feel
a wind & rain whips across
the Indians' apple orchard.

Sighting far off we find a white speck;
it's James Fenimore Cooper composing
a novel entitled *The Chainbearer.*
He's been following us in his
white linen suit & black baseball cap with
"Syracuse Chiefs" stitched in orange
across the front, the team formed by
Abner Doubleday, the inventor of folklore, &
Lewis Henry Morgan, the discoverer of Masonic Indians.
My hat shows a flying ear of corn
symbolizing the Iroquois flight to Canada.
They crossed on dry land at Niagara Falls.

Now it's my turn to hold the rod
while George counts out the land.
Boundaries proceed from eye judgements,
to lines in our head, to marks on a map
which people may live within.
Finally we suggest that this place
be called Homer & that Ovid.
Populations of veterans rush in
to claim the land but like Vandals
don't know how to pronounce the names.
We go to work on the road west
which takes off over the hills.

Other Individual Poets

Alta, *i am not a practicing angel*, $3.95
Elliott, Harley, *All Beautyfull & Foolish Souls*, $2.95
Gill, John, *Country Pleasures*, $4.95
Hazard, James, *A Hive of Souls*, $3.95
Hershon, Robert, *Grocery Lists*, $2.95
Hilton, David, *Huladance*, $2.95
Lifshin, Lyn, *Black Apples*, $3. 95
——————————, *Upstate Madonna*, $4.95
Lindquist, Ray, *By-Products*, $3.00
Lourie, Dick, *Stumbling*, $3.95
McCarthy, Gerald, *War Story*, $2.95
McCord, Howard, *Selected Poems*, $4.95
——————————, *The Great Toad Hunt &
Other Expeditions*, $3.95
Peters, Robert, *Gauguin's Chair: Selected Poems,
1967-1974*, $4.95
Wiegner, Kathleen, *Country Western Breakdown*, $2.95
Young, Ian, *Double Exposure*, $2.50

available from your bookstore or from
The Crossing Press, Trumansburg, N.Y. 14886